# Momma
# Is Daddy
# Going to Hell?

**Tyrone
Short**

# TABLE OF CONTENTS

Introduction                                          5

Momma is Daddy Going to Hell?                         13

Epilogue                                             100

Are You Truly a Child of God or Are You a Candidate for
Hell Exam                                            102

Answer Key                                           122

Final Words                                          139

About the Author                                     132

Little Johnny got up early Sunday morning, however this was not just any Sunday morning, this was Little Johnny's first trip to church. Little Johnny was excited as his mother dressed him up in the cutest little suit.

Little Johnny:       Momma, how do I look?

Momma:              You look incredibly handsome.

Little Johnny:       Momma, am I a handsome man?

Momma:              Yes Little Johnny, you are a handsome young man.

Little Johnny:       Momma, can I tie my own tie?

Momma:              My dear child, let me do it for you before you mess it up?

Little Johnny:       Momma I can do it!

Momma:              Go ahead baby; let me see you do it.

Little Johnny, named after his father, tried diligently to tie his tie. After watching Little Johnny try in vain, his mother finally suited him up and drove him to his first church service.

Little Johnny, a product of divorce, has been living with his father for the first couple of years after the divorce, because the judge felt that his mother was not financially stable enough to allow him to live with her full-time.

Little Johnny's mother, originally being brought up in a Christian household, had fell into a backslidden state, to include marrying Big Johnny, Little Johnny's father. However, due to the divorce, Little Johnny's mother found herself seeking the Lord's face. Whereas, Big Johnny's home did not serve the Lord.

Little Johnny was excited to walk into the church for his first time and see many other little boys his age dressed up in suits. He was happy to see his mother's expression as she singed joyfully as the choir played. Because of his young age he has no memory of seeing his mother this happy. All he remembers is seeing her crying when she drops him back off at his father's place after weekend visitation.

Meanwhile back at church, as the choir was coming to a close on the last song, Pastor Scott made his way to the altar.

Pastor Scott: Salvation is available to all. A relationship with God is available to all. In John 3 it says, 'For God so loved the world that He gave His one and only Son, that whoever believes in him shall not perish but have eternal life. For God did not send His Son into the world to condemn the world, but to save the world through Him. Whoever believes in Him is not condemned, but whoever does not believe stands condemned already because he has not believed in the name of God's one and only Son.' Salvation is available to all. A relationship with God is available to all. But for only those who believe in the one and only son of God. They will spend eternity with Him in Heaven. But for those who don't believe in God's one and only Son, they will spend eternity in HELL.

These words ranged through the head of Little Johnny. He has never heard of this son of God. He has never heard of Heaven. He has never heard of Hell.

Within the next couple of months, Little Johnny had many opportunities to go with his mother to church. No longer was he excited about his dress attire. No longer was he overwhelmed to see his mother happy as she singed joyously. Little Johnny instead sat intently listening to what Pastor Scott had to say about this dreadful place called Hell.

Thus came the day that Little Johnny's mother had not expected. Thus came the day that Little Johnny's mother had not prepared for. Thus came the day that Little Johnny's mother had to allow the Holy Spirit of Christ to lead her in answering questions that will be a stumbling block for many:

Little Johnny:     Momma is daddy going to Hell?

Momma Is Daddy Going to Hell?

By Tyrone Short

Printed in the United States of America

ISBN   978-0-6152-4502-7    2008

Scripture taken from the HOLY BIBLE, NEW
INTERNATIONAL VERSION ®.  Copyright ©
1973, 1978, and 1984 by International Bible
Society.  Used by permission of Zondervan
Publishing House.  All rights reserved.

Lulu Publishing
Www.Lulu.com

Is Little Johnny's father going to Hell?  Why was Hell created?  Why should we as a society be concerned about Hell?

If your child is not asking now, will you be ready later?  Are you prepared to answer those questions that every child wants to know about Hell?

'Momma Is Daddy Going to Hell?' is a collection of some of the most provocative questions your child may ask about Hell and God.  In today's times of false and heretical teachings, Christian parents must be prepared to answer these questions.

They must be answered delicately.  They must be answered tactfully.  Moreover, they must be answered biblically.

Momma is daddy going to Hell?  He doesn't go to church and he used to hit you a lot and God hates divorce and daddy divorced you.

My dear child, God's love and mercy will cover over the multitude of sins that is committed by any being. However what is required by that person is to confess his sins to the Lord, repent of those sins and to accept Jesus Christ as his Lord and Savior and he will be saved.

God loves your father more than I ever could. Until your father seeks the Lord's face in regards to what he has done, he is at God's mercy.

# Momma why are church people going to Hell?

My dear child, the Lord says in **Matthew 7:22-23**:

"Many will say to me on that day, 'Lord, Lord, did we not prophesy in your name and in your name drive out demons and perform many miracles?' Then I will tell them plainly, 'I never knew you. Away from me, you evildoers!'

What He was saying there was that there are many people who profess to know the Lord or profess to be Christians. However, Jesus is saying that they are not. This is reflective with what we have come to know as 'church people', many who have become religious, but have not been born again by the Holy Spirit.

Today there are many church people who are not born again. They play in the choir. They serve as ushers. Dreadfully, some of them even serve as pastors. Nevertheless, there is no difference between them and the unbeliever.

Some came because they loved the music. Some came because they loved the community. Some came because they became religious. For some unfortunately, they refused to repent of their old sins.

Nevertheless, because of the fact that they did not examine themselves to see if they were truly in the faith, they will die and go to Hell.

Momma what about Mrs. Smith who works at the hospital?  She has spent her whole life helping people.  But when I tell her my mommy and daddy are Christians, she says, "That's nice".  Is she going to Hell?

My dear child, if Mrs. Smith refuses to recognize that Jesus Christ is the creator of all things, the creator of the heavens and earth, the Almighty God, the King of Kings, the Lord of Lords, and the author of her faith, then she will perish and go to Hell. It is not her good works that will save her. For as it says in **Ephesians 2:8:**

For it is by grace you have been saved, through faith – and this not from yourselves, it is the gift of God – not by works, so that no one can boast.

Unless Mrs. Smith repents and come into knowledge of this truth, she will not be saved from the wrath of God.

Momma if Mrs. Smith goes to Hell and then asks God to forgive her, can she then come to Heaven to be with us?

My dear child, the answer is no, because between those who will reside in Heaven and those who will reside in Hell, a great chasm has been fixed, so that those who want to go from Hell to Heaven won't be able to cross over. It is also written in **Hebrews 9:27:**

Just as man is destined to die once, and after that to face judgment …

In other words, at the time of Mrs. Smith's death, if she has not come into a right relationship with the Lord, it will be too late to change her mind.

# Momma why does God send good people to Hell?

My dear child, God does not send good people to Hell. For it is God's desire that all men be saved and come to a knowledge of the truth. However, due to God's grace of allowing us to have free will, many of us choose to suppress the truth oppose to accepting and embracing it. God has allowed men to carry their free will into the kindest of deeds, as well as the darkest of sins. With God's grace and patience, He allows them to live another day, desiring for them to repent. For even the kindest of deeds by the kindest of people can equate to filthy rags in His eyes.

Nevertheless, it is their sin of unbelief in Him that will keep them out of His glorious presence. After all, why should He allow someone who doesn't believe in Him to spend eternity with Him? And for those who joyfully pursue the quest to sin, God's grace to allow their free will to rule does not include allowing them to bring their wickedness into Heaven.

# Momma why does God allow bad teaching in His churches?

My dear child, God had said while He walked the earth, that we should not try to separate the tare from the wheat because in doing so we may uproot some of the wheat. Furthermore, the allowance of false teachings in the churches enables His sheep to be challenged, and then to challenge. False teaching challenges His children to examine the scriptures to see if what these preachers are teaching are credible, thus allowing them to grow and then challenge these false teachers that come into their churches.

When His children respond in this way they protect themselves from falling prey to every new teaching under the sun.

Momma
can a woman who
becomes a man or a
man who becomes a
woman go to hell?

My dear child, a person who commits to such a lifestyle change and believes that they are in a right relationship with God is terribly deceived.

A commitment such as this shows a lack of gratitude for what God has created them to be. It also tells God that they are the ones that are in control of their lives. It also tells God that they have no fear of the consequences of what He had called an abomination.

Churches turned cults such as the Episcopal Church have deceived many into thinking that God approves of gender changes and homosexual relationships. They have gone as far as allowing these beings to marry within the walls of their church. They have even gone as putting some of these beings into positions of authority. Churches such as this will be held accountable for their actions.

God loves these beings dearly and desires for them to come into a right relationship with Him. But unless they repent, they will die and go to Hell.

Momma will all the bad people get together and say bad things about God in Hell?

My dear child, as illustrated in the story entitled, 'The Rich Man and Lazarus', in Luke 16, while the rich man resided in Hell, he was all alone. He may have had the option to curse God, like many others do and will have over the generations; however, they will do it all alone. Unfortunate for those in Hell, one of the biggest torments they will face is eternal isolation.

Momma how does God know the difference between Christians and Church People?

My dear child, God knows all.  God is omniscient, meaning God is all-knowing.  God knows the hearts of men, because He seeks it out.  Therefore, He knows those who diligently seek Him, love Him and have truly put their faith and trust in Him for salvation and all.

He also knows those who have sat in the church for years refusing to repent, exploiting His children, always seeking but never finding, becoming enlightened and tasting the heavenly gift, sharing in the Holy Spirit, and tasting the goodness of the word of God, but still refusing to open the door.

# Momma if a person commits suicide will he go to Hell?

My dear child, suicide is not the unpardonable sin. Moreover, because of the poor choices and sins that we have allowed to dwell in our lives, suicide has become the completed project and the final release of our deteriorated status and earthly bodies.

Many well meaning Christians condemn suicide as a lack of faith. Where this may be applicable for a person who is going through a bankruptcy or one who just broke up with a girlfriend, however, grace should be applied to those with long term, painful and terminal diseases.

# Momma can a Christian go to Hell if he belongs to a cult?

My dear child, God allows us into Heaven because of coming into submission of a knowledge of Him, and allows grace to cover us in those other things that we have a lack of knowledge in.

In reference to cults, as we all know there are some cults which are more problematic than others.

There are Christian cults and non-Christian cults.

The Christian cults are labeled as such because they have embraced the biblical essentials of the gospel, however due to sin and erroneous teaching; they believe things such as; that they are the only true church. Churches such as the International Church of Christ have polluted minds with this lie for decades.

The Non-Christian cults are labeled as such because they deny the deity of Jesus Christ. Jehovah's Witnesses, Mormons and groups such as this claim to be Christian; however they preach a false gospel and tell lies inspired by false prophets.

A true born-again Christian who has aligned himself with a Christian cult will grieve the spirit that lives inside of him, due to his acceptance of erroneous teachings. Churches such as these put more precedence in winning bodies to their church than souls to Christ.

For the many that are saved within the walls of churches such as these, they will one day come into the reality that they did not keep the unity of the Spirit, they brought division into the kingdom, and they shall be held accountable for their manipulative and controlling teachings with few if any rewards.

A true born-again Christian who has aligned himself with a non-Christian cult will grieve the spirit that lives inside of him, due to his acceptance of erroneous teachings that blaspheme the name of God. Churches such as these refuse to acknowledge Jesus Christ for who he was, God in the flesh. However, they wish to blaspheme His holy name by calling Jesus Christ the half-brother of Lucifer, by calling God a former man, and by taking away divinity from Jesus Christ.

God had a son, and His name was Jesus Christ. There were many prophets, but Muhammad was not one of them. Neither was Buddha, Joseph Smith, Charles Taze Russell or Sun Young Moon. These men were deceived and have deceived many.

For the many people that are serving with the walls of non-Christian churches such as these, they will one day come into the reality that since they did not believe that Jesus Christ was who He claimed to be, they will die in their sins.

Momma Oprah Winfrey says that there are many paths to God, is this true and if so are there many paths to Hell?

My dear child, Oprah Winfrey has been deceived. She has been deceived and is using her platform to deceive others with the assistance of her New Age Teachers.

In Oprah Winfrey's defense, she has done many wonderful things in her time. However, the many wonderful things that she has done for people on this earth will amount to nothing for them if they perish and go to Hell.

Jesus Christ says in **John 14:6:**

I am the way, and the truth, and the life; no one comes to the Father but through me.

Jesus Christ was known for healing many of their diseases and illnesses. Jesus Christ was known for ridding people of demons. Jesus Christ was known for turning water into wine. Jesus Christ was known for walking on water. Jesus Christ was known for feeding thousands with just seven loaves of bread and a few small fish. Jesus Christ was known for raising the dead.

My dear child, who would you rather believe; Jesus Christ or Oprah Winfrey?

And yes, my dear child, there are many paths to Hell.

Momma some people have written books about how they died and went to Hell and then said they saw the devil, is this true?

My dear child, no matter how sincere these men pose to be, but the reality is that these men are sincerely wrong. The Bible teaches that the devil is currently the prince of this world and is prowling around like a roaring lion looking for someone to devour, and that his time to fall has been predestined for, therefore the devil is currently not, nor has been in hell.

Secondly, in regards to these writers who have claimed to have died and seen hell, these men are liars or have been deceived. The Bible teaches that there is a great chasm that is fixed that separates those that reside in that realm from any other physical or spiritual realm (**Luke 16**).

Therefore my dear child, if the world was not persuaded by the historical account of Jesus of Nazareth, who was crucified, who was buried and has risen from the grave, why should they believe these liars and men who have been deceived?

# Momma will there be famous people and celebrities in hell?

My dear child, there will be in hell people from all walks of life. There will be famous and non-famous, rich and poor, successful and non-successful, celebrities and non-celebrities, weak and strong.

The scriptures teach that God has taken the foolish of the world to shame the wise, and the weak to bring shame to the strong.

Many of the wise and strong people according to the world's standards are famous or successful. Whether movie stars, singers, famous politicians, comedians or athletes, many of these men and women are notorious for blasphemy against the name of the Lord.

Throughout Hollywood, many give thanks to the Lord for the gift of writing books, singing songs and performing in roles that are as unholy and unrighteous as anything you have ever seen or heard. Sadly enough, many of them credit God for the ability to commit these blasphemies. Movie stars who have played roles in rated 'R' movies filled with profanity, nude scenes and senseless violence, have thanked God for their awards. As absurd as it may sound, but porn stars have even taken the stage and have thanked God for being able to commit the lewd things that they do.

Ironically, we recently had one comedian, Kathy Griffin; make a public declaration of not having to thank Jesus for the award that she had received, even going as far as making a derogatory remark towards Him. This woman obviously has no fear or reverence of God. The audience should have walked out on her because of the evilness that lives within her.

Nevertheless, there are many of other celebrities and shows that mock the name of God regularly. They create shows that make a mockery of Him as a cartoon character such as South Park. They do comical sketches of what is supposed to be hilarious prayer scenes such as Talladega Nights: The Ballad of Ricky Bobby. Moreover, they even play roles that they are God.

Many of these actors and actresses many bring countless of hours of entertainment to the big screens and some of our households, however, unless they repent, they will die and go to Hell.

# Momma is there such a thing as 'Hell on earth'?

My dear child, there is no hell on earth. In spite of the many trials and tribulations that men may face on earth, these trials are going to pale in comparison with what they are going to face in hell.

In all my years on this earth, I do not recall anyone being thrown into a lake of fire or go into an unquenchable fire where their worm does not die, and the fire is not quenched.

Therefore, whether it's financial, physical or sexual abuse, physical or mental illness, or any other crime, plague or situation known to man, the hell that will fall upon the lost and fallen man will surpass anything that they will experience on this earth because it will be exceedingly tormenting and everlasting.

Momma if Hell is real, why don't they talk about it in many churches?

My dear child, Hell is not talked about much in churches anymore because we are experiencing a taste of the great apostasy.

The Holy Scriptures warns us in **2 Timothy 3** of a great falling away in the last days. In these last days, men will be lovers of anything but God and will oppose the truth. These men who oppose the truth will gain positions of authority in the church, leading people away from anything that they consider offensive or in contrast with what makes them feel good.

**2 Timothy 4:3**

For the time will come when they will not endure sound doctrine; but wanting to have their ears tickled, they will accumulate for themselves teachers in accordance to their own desires.

They will deceive many into believing that Hell does not exist and that all will be saved, false teachers such as Carlton Pearson are lurking through the churches today.

These men will take away words from the Holy Scriptures, and not only will God prove them to be liars, but they will lose their share in the tree of life and in the Holy City.

Momma if you murder somebody will you automatically go to Hell?

My dear child, murder is not the unforgivable sin. As horrible and wicked a crime murder may be; it is not the sin that leads to death.

There are men who were former fornicators, idolaters, adulterers, homosexuals, thieves, drunkards, and even murderers, who have given up their former lifestyles and have come to know the Lord. Many of these men are now productive members in the Kingdom of God, holding positions such as evangelists, pastors, choir leaders and missionaries, living a life of repentance evidenced by action.

So my dear child, there will be former murderers in heaven, for the only unforgivable sin is the sin of unbelief.

Momma if someone believes in God but doesn't believe in the Bible, will they go to Hell?

My dear child, many will say that they believe in God, only holding to a form of godliness but denying its power. However, to claim to believe in God, but not believe in His word, will equate to calling Him a liar.

For generations, many men have tried to disprove the validity of God's written word, and have failed tremendously. If this man who claims to believe in God, however denies His word, then from where does this person derive his understanding of God? From where does he derive his teaching and spiritual direction from?

I would boldly say that if this person is instructed from any other book outside of the Holy Scriptures, from books such as 'The Secret' by Rhonda Byrne, then more than likely it is a teaching from the pit of hell.

This man who claims to believe in God will die and go to hell like the demons that also believe in God but do not abide by His word.

Momma where are more people going, to Heaven or to Hell?

My dear child, as painful as it is for me to say this, but there will be many more who will die and go to Hell than there are people who will die and go to Heaven.

The Holy Scriptures teach that the gate is wide and the road is broad that leads to destruction, and many enter through it. But small is the gate and narrow the road that leads to life (Heaven) and only a few find it.

In all reality, my dear child, you will know more people in your lifetime that will go to Hell than you will know people that will go to Heaven.

# Momma is it really hot in hell?

My dear child, the Holy Scriptures refer to the rich man in **Luke 16** as being in agony in the fire.  However, many Bible teachers and commentators have taught for generations that the fire could just be an analogy referring to a strong and burning grief stricken state.

Looking at it from the natural and fleshly eyes, you would believe that this man would just burn up in the flames and be no more.  However, since this is a spiritual connotation, one would believe that the grief stricken state would be closer to the truth since spiritual death is the separation of the soul from God.

Momma if scientists are so smart why don't they believe in Hell?

My dear child, scientists have contributed enormously to the advancement of human civilization. However, their vast knowledge of biology, chemistry, geology and the likes, does not equate to spiritual knowledge.

The grace of God has gifted many men with many natural gifts; however some have become fools and have used these gifts to try to disprove the existence of God. Nevertheless, for the many of these scientists who may spend years of their studies trying to discredit the Bible and the existence of God, they will one day find themselves bowing and calling out for His mercy.

# Momma does the devil want to go to Hell?

My dear child, the devil does not want to go hell, but his pride keeps him from any other fate.

It was due to the devil's pride in the beginning that caused him to be casted down from Heaven. He wanted to raise his throne above God's own throne.

Now he has been banished to roam the earth until the appointed day in which he will be thrown in to the lake of burning sulfur, where he will be tormented day and night.

When the devil tempted Jesus in the desert, his plan was thwarted by scriptures, this is because the devil knows the scriptures and his destruction, but his pride has marked his inability to repent.

# Momma are any of your friends going to Hell?

My dear child, it pains me deeply to say this, but the answer is yes.

I love all of my friends dearly, and many of them I have known since I was an early teen. However, some of them have not allowed Jesus Christ to be the Lord over their lives.

In spite of my decision to follow Christ, and their decisions not to, we still remain friends. Now of course, some of those friendships have become hampered, whether through moral or legal issues, but I still love them dearly.

The greatest love I can give them as a friend is to continue to share the good news of Jesus Christ.

Momma what about the people who never heard of Hell do they go to Hell when they die?

My dear child, it is not a matter if they heard of Hell or not, it is a matter of what they did with what God has made plain to them.

Not everyone who has lived has heard of Hell, has heard the name of Jesus Christ, has seen a Bible, or has heard the term God. However, God has revealed to all of mankind His existence as explained in **Romans I**.

Whether or not they have heard of Hell, if they have not accepted the light that God has revealed to them and then followed that path to salvation, then Hell will one day become real to them.

Momma should a person who is going to Heaven marry a person who is going to Hell?

My dear child, for one who is aspiring to go to Heaven and be with the Lord, that person should not engage in a romantic relationship with someone who is not aspiring to do the same.

**2 Corinthians 6** warns us as Christians that we shouldn't be unequally yoked. God calls us to separate ourselves from them because we have nothing in common with them. A marriage such as that will continuously go through spiritual unrest, for the devil will always influence the unbelieving party to be at war with the believing party. They could never be soul mates as the world knows it.

# Momma will there be kids in Hell?

My dear child, Hell will be foreign to the sight of precious and darling kids such as you.

Jesus says that the Kingdom of God belongs to kids like you.

The Holy Scriptures teach us that the children, who do not yet know good from bad, will enter the land. It is not until each child reaches his age of accountability, will he be held accountable for that sin that leads to death.

# Momma will there be pets in Hell?

My dear child, there is no biblical evidence to believe that there will be pets in Heaven or Hell.

Many of us would love to believe that our family pets that we have formed strong relationships with, will one day be in Heaven, however there is no reason to believe that animals have spirits.

Moreover, in the eternal scheme of things, it is the children of God that the Lord wishes to redeem most, and pets are not children of God.

# Momma will there be angels in Hell?

My dear child, there will definitely be angels in Hell. The Bible teaches that the devil was once an angel who led other angels in a revolt to take over Heaven, but failed and was then casted out. The Bible then mentions how Hell has been reserved for the devil and his dominions.

Unfortunately, as much as it displeases God, many of mankind will be joining them.

## Epilogue:

Three years later, Big Johnny died. In Hell, where he was in torment, he thought of his son Little Johnny.

Big Johnny died almost 3 years after Little Johnny first asked the question to his mother, "Momma is daddy going to Hell?" He was shot in the back while laying with his mistress. For jealousy had aroused the fury of the husband of Big Johnny's mistress, and he had shown no mercy when he took revenge.

Momma, in spite of her awareness of Big Johnny's bouts with infidelity, had truly loved her husband. She has since become the leader of the single mother's ministry at the church.

Little Johnny, also aware of his father's infidelity, missed his father dearly. After becoming aware of the good news of Jesus Christ, Little Johnny has devoted his life to the Lord and has become a Christian rapper spreading the good new of the gospel to the lost.

## Are You Truly a Child of God or Are You Destined for Hell Exam?

-        This quiz contains 110 multiple choice questions, each worth 1 point.

-        There are 10 questions that if answered incorrectly are an automatic failure.

-        A score of 70 is required for a passing grade.

-        There is no time limit to finish the test.

This exam is worth a total of 100 points.  *Good Luck!!*


## HONOR PLEDGE FOR THIS EXAM:

I pledge that I am answering these questions with all honesty and integrity to reflect how I truly feel and what I will truly do, and I will not answer based on what I believe is what the correct answer is.

I pledge that I will not look up the answers to the exam prior to taking the exam, especially to find out which of the 110 questions are the automatic failures.

1)   Do you have a secret sin in your life that you have been struggling with for years?

( ) Yes  ( ) No

2)   Do you have a church that you consistently attend?

( ) Yes  ( ) No

3)   Do you daily grow closer to the Lord with devotional prayer and biblical reading?

( ) Yes  ( ) No

4)   Since becoming a Christian, do you find yourself becoming more attracted to music that glorifies God and touches the soul rather than music of the world such as rap, rock, R&B, jazz, blues, reggae, etc…?

( ) Yes  ( ) No

5)   Can you truly say that you love God with all your heart & soul?

( ) Yes  ( ) No

6)   Do you look forward to the return of Christ?

( ) Yes  ( ) No

7)   Do you look forward to fellowshipping with other saints?

( ) Yes  ( ) No

8) Do you have a hatred for the Jews?

( ) Yes ( ) No

9) Do you find yourself speaking derogatorily of others?

( ) Yes ( ) No

10) Do you believe that Jesus Christ is God?

( ) Yes ( ) No

11) Do you follow the horoscopes?

( ) Yes ( ) No

12) Is it important to you to keep Sunday as a day of worship, and work only if necessary?

( ) Yes ( ) No

13) Do you believe that the only allowance for divorce should be adultery, physical abuse and abandonment?

( ) Yes ( ) No

14) Since becoming a Christian do the people in your life notice the change for righteousness?

( ) Yes ( ) No

15) When trying to prove your word do you swear in the name of God?

( ) Yes ( ) No

16) Do you utilize your spiritual gifts to benefit God's kingdom?

( ) Yes ( ) No

17) Do you have no problem in marking up the price of an item you are selling to gain a profit?

( ) Yes ( ) No

18) Do you owe money to anyone or an organization that you refuse to pay back?

( ) Yes ( ) No

19) If you are or were single would you marry an unbeliever?

( ) Yes ( ) No

20) Do you believe that Jesus Christ died for your sins, that He was buried, and that he was raised on the third day?

( ) Yes ( ) No

21)    Regardless if you believe that tithing is biblical for today, do you regularly donate money to the advancement of God's Kingdom?

( ) Yes  ( )  No

22)    If you are or were single would you date or marry someone outside your own race?

( ) Yes  ( )  No

23)    Do you struggle in forgiving someone who has wronged you?

( ) Yes  ( )  No

24)    Are there people in your life who you refuse to ever forgive?

( ) Yes  ( )  No

25)    Do you believe that it is appropriate to have sex before marriage?

( ) Yes  ( )  No

26)    Since becoming a Christian have you ever led anyone to Christ?

( ) Yes  ( )  No

27) Do you have compassion for the homeless to the extent that you give them money when led by the Lord?

( ) Yes ( ) No

28) When trouble and stressful events come into your life, are you able to find inner peace?

( ) Yes ( ) No

29) Do you have a prayer life which consists of prayers devoted to praise and thanks even when you do not find yourself in trouble or in need of anything?

( ) Yes ( ) No

30) Do you believe that you are saved by faith alone and not by your works?

( ) Yes ( ) No

31) Do you recognize the voice of God?

( ) Yes ( ) No

32) Are you involved in any ministry work?

( ) Yes ( ) No

33) Are you storing up for yourself treasures in Heaven?

( ) Yes ( ) No

34)   Since becoming a Christian do you now find yourself struggling to watch a rated 'R' movie because of the profanity, nudity and violence?

( ) Yes  ( )  No

35)   Since becoming a Christian are you seeing God working in your life by answering prayers?

( ) Yes  ( )  No

36)   Do you find yourself regularly denying Christ?

( ) Yes  ( )  No

37)   Do you normally lie to get out of a bad situation?

( ) Yes  ( )  No

38)   Are there scriptures that you have memorized to help you against your temptations from Satan?

( ) Yes  ( )  No

39)   Do you ever spend time with God in silent prayer in the hopes of hearing from Him when there is no trouble, discord or prayers that need to be answered in your life?

( ) Yes  ( )  No

40)   Do you believe that there is more than one way to Heaven?

( ) Yes  ( )  No

41)   Is it more important that God's will for your life be done than your own happiness?

( ) Yes  ( ) No

42)   Do you believe that all religions point to the same God?

( ) Yes  ( ) No

43)   Do you have any people in your life that you disciple?

( ) Yes  ( ) No

44)   Do you work at your place of employment as if you were working for the Lord?

( ) Yes  ( ) No

45)   Do you believe that everyone's belief should be their own private matter?

( ) Yes  ( ) No

46)   Do you believe that it is okay to live with someone of the opposite sex prior to marriage?

( ) Yes  ( ) No

47)   Do you believe that getting baptized was essential to your walk with Christ?

( ) Yes  ( ) No

48)   Since becoming a Christian has the Bible become or is becoming one of your most read books?

( ) Yes  ( ) No

49)   Do you have a burning desire to reach the lost loved ones in your life?

( ) Yes  ( ) No

50)   Do you believe that the Bible is the inerrant word of God?

( ) Yes  ( ) No

51)   Are you able to intelligently and scripturally contend for the faith?

( ) Yes  ( ) No

52)   Are you at peace when you hear sermons on hell & judgment oppose to a spiritual unrest?

( ) Yes  ( ) No

53) Do the people closest to you recognize you as a man or woman of God?

( ) Yes ( ) No

54) Would you be ashamed or embarrassed if your church knew what shows you watched at night on television?

( ) Yes ( ) No

55) Do you fear death?

( ) Yes ( ) No

56 Do you pray to the dead for guidance?

( ) Yes ( ) No

57 Do you observe communion as part of your worship?

( ) Yes ( ) No

58 Do you believe that it is necessary to confess your sins to God to stay in a right communion with Him?

( ) Yes ( ) No

59 Is there a sin in your life that you refuse to let go?

( ) Yes ( ) No

60    Are you in need of a Savior?

( ) Yes  ( ) No

61    Do you love your enemy?

( ) Yes  ( ) No

62    Are you willing to be martyred for Jesus Christ?

( ) Yes  ( ) No

63    Do you find yourself debating the word of God more than you find yourself sharing the word of God?

( ) Yes  ( ) No

64    Are you willing to work in the lowest position in the smallest of churches to serve the Lord?

( ) Yes  ( ) No

65    Are you more attracted to the names and lifestyles of Hollywood stars than the names and lifestyles of Biblical Heroes?

( ) Yes  ( ) No

66    Is there anyone you personally owe an apology, but you refuse to give it to them?

( ) Yes  ( ) No

67     Is there anyone you personally owe money, but you refuse to give it to them?

( ) Yes ( ) No

68     Do you pray for the salvation of those that have wronged you?

( ) Yes ( ) No

69     Can you honestly say that you love God even when times are bad?

( ) Yes ( ) No

70     Do you believe that Jesus Christ was just a good man or a teacher?

( ) Yes ( ) No

71     Do you try to read the Bible daily?

( ) Yes ( ) No

72     Do you pray daily?

( ) Yes ( ) No

73     Do you believe that churches should be segregated by people of different race and color?

( ) Yes ( ) No

74     Do you believe that everyone will be saved?

( ) Yes  ( ) No

75     Do you believe that false teachers have infiltrated the church?

( ) Yes  ( ) No

76     Do you believe that the church will one day be raptured?

( ) Yes  ( ) No

77     Do you believe that it is okay for a Christian to smoke cigarettes?

( ) Yes  ( ) No

78     Do you believe that it is okay for a Christian to watch pornography?

( ) Yes  ( ) No

79     Do you believe that you could lose your salvation?

( ) Yes  ( ) No

80     Did you receive the Holy Spirit when you gave your life to God?

( ) Yes  ( ) No

81    Do you believe that Jesus Christ was fully God and fully man?

( ) Yes  ( ) No

82    Do you believe that you deserve to go to Heaven?

( ) Yes  ( ) No

83    Can you praise God even when you are suffering?

( ) Yes  ( ) No

84    Do you have a person or people in your life that you hold yourself accountable to outside of Jesus Christ to share your victories and struggles and to help you overcome those secret sins?

( ) Yes  ( ) No

85    Do you believe that all of your money belongs to the Lord?

( ) Yes  ( ) No

86    Do you believe in the concept of the Trinity?

( ) Yes  ( ) No

87    Do you believe in purgatory?

( ) Yes  ( ) No

88    Do you love God more than you love your own wife/husband/son/daughter?

( ) Yes  ( ) No


89    Can you have Jesus Christ as your savior, but not your Lord?

( ) Yes  ( ) No


90    Before giving your life to God, were you a sinner worthy of going to Hell?

( ) Yes  ( ) No


91    Do you fear God?

( ) Yes  ( ) No


92    Do you believe in creationism?

( ) Yes  ( ) No


93    Do you believe that Christians should judge the teachings of all biblical teachers and pastors?

( ) Yes  ( ) No


94    Do you believe that you are called to honor God with your body?

( ) Yes  ( ) No

95   Do you believe that God is in control over everything that happens under the sun?

( ) Yes  ( )  No

96   Do you believe that Israel is God's chosen nation?

( ) Yes  ( )  No

97   Do you believe that God is holy and that you are called to live a life that is holy as well?

( ) Yes  ( )  No

98   Do you believe that God has a plan for Israel?

( ) Yes  ( )  No

99   Do you thank God even when prayers are not answered?

( ) Yes  ( )  No

100   Do you believe that Jesus Christ was just another prophet?

( ) Yes  ( )  No

101   Do you belong to a church that has a reputation for being known as a cult?

( ) Yes  ( )  No

102    Do you support a woman's right to have an abortion?

( ) Yes  ( ) No

103    Do you believe that there are some absolute truths?

( ) Yes  ( ) No

104    Should a child of God pray with people of other faiths and religions?

( ) Yes  ( ) No

105    Do you believe that your lack of faith can hinder God's will?

( ) Yes  ( ) No

106    Do you have a problem controlling your anger?

( ) Yes  ( ) No

107    Do you obey God and keep His requirements, His commands, His decrees and His laws?

( ) Yes  ( ) No

108    Are there scriptures that you have memorized to help you evangelize to the lost?

( ) Yes  ( ) No

109    Do you ever fast to focus your mind on God and His will?

( ) Yes  ( ) No

110    Do you have a pastor or a teacher who has a reputation as being known as a false teacher?

( ) Yes  ( ) No

# Answer Key for Quiz

1)      N
2)      Y
3)      Y
4)      Y
5)      Y
6)      Y
7)      Y
8)      N
9)      N
10)     AN ANSWER OF 'NO' RESULTS IN AN AUTOMATIC FAILURE
11)     N
12)     Y
13)     Y
14)     Y
15)     N
16)     Y
17)     N
18)     N
19)     N
20)     AN ANSWER OF 'NO' RESULTS IN AN AUTOMATIC FAILURE
21)     Y
22)     Y
23)     N
24)     N
25)     N
26)     Y
27)     Y
28)     Y
29)     Y

30)     AN ANSWER OF 'NO' RESULTS IN AN
    AUTOMATIC FAILURE
31)     Y
32)     Y
33)     Y
34)     Y
35)     Y
36)     N
37)     N
38)     Y
39)     Y
40)     AN ANSWER OF 'YES' RESULTS IN AN
    AUTOMATIC FAILURE
41)     Y
42)     N
43)     Y
44)     Y
45)     N
46)     N
47)     Y
48)     Y
49)     Y
50)     AN ANSWER OF 'NO' RESULTS IN AN
    AUTOMATIC FAILURE
51)     Y
52)     Y
53)     Y
54)     N
55)     N
56)     N
57)     Y
58)     Y
59)     N

60) AN ANSWER OF 'NO' RESULTS IN AN AUTOMATIC FAILURE
61) Y
62) Y
63) N
64) Y
65) N
66) N
67) N
68) Y
69) Y
70) AN ANSWER OF 'YES' RESULTS IN AN AUTOMATIC FAILURE
71) Y
72) Y
73) N
74) N
75) Y
76) Y
77) N
78) N
79) N
80) AN ANSWER OF 'NO' RESULTS IN AN AUTOMATIC FAILURE
81) Y
82) N
83) Y
84) Y
85) Y
86) Y
87) N
88) Y
89) N

90) AN ANSWER OF 'NO' RESULTS IN AN
AUTOMATIC FAILURE
91) Y
92) Y
93) Y
94) Y
95) Y
96) Y
97) Y
98) Y
99) Y
100) AN ANSWER OF 'YES' RESULTS IN AN
AUTOMATIC FAILURE
101) N
102) N
103) Y
104) N
105) N
106) N
107) Y
108) Y
109) Y
110) N

Congratulations, you have finished the exam. As stated in the beginning of the exam, there are 10 questions that if answered incorrectly are an automatic failure. Those questions are 10, 20, 30, 40, 50, 60, 70, 80, 90 and 100. If you answered 'no' to any of these questions, you have failed the test and are not a Christian. You would want to speak to your pastor or another Christian to go over these questions with him.

In reference to the other questions, add up every question that you answered correctly, each worth one point, thus giving you your final score.

*** It is important to know that any grade of 68 and lower does not definitely mean that you are not a Christian, but it may mean that Jesus Christ is not your first priority, and you may want to examine your heart to see if Jesus Christ truly lives inside of you. As well as a passing mark of 70 or higher does not necessarily mean that you are truly born again by the Holy Spirit. For there is no way to possibly measure the spiritual with the flesh. However, if you scored less than 30, there is a grave concern that you are not a true Christian. Please use this as a litmus test to see where you are in your walk with Jesus Christ. ***

There are many books, teachings and sermons available regarding Hell. Moreover, there are many opinions regarding the subject, some close to the truth and many that are far from it. Nevertheless, the truth still remains, that Hell will become a reality and a home for many.

No longer will these men have joy. No longer will these men smile. No longer will these men walk around snubbing their noses at God. No longer will these men be allowed to explore and taste every evil under the sun.

No longer will church people be able to occupy pews and be entertained with music that glorifies the Lord, while in their hearts they bargain with the level of repentance they are willing to release. No longer well these men sing, serve and teach in God's house, while meanwhile they were neither appointed or was it in God's will.

No longer will Hollywood be allowed to thank God under one breath and then curse Him under another. No longer will scientists be allowed to try and devise ideas and theories why He doesn't exist. No longer will atheists be allowed to speak behind soapboxes and write books trying to explain away His existence. No longer will the public schools and the city, state and government institutions be allowed to cast His name from their thresholds.

How the many have rejected the Almighty, the Omnipresent, the Omnipotent, the Omniscient, King of Kings, Lord of Lords, Mighty Conquering Lion of the Tribe of Judah, so they will be rejected by Him.

They will die.  They will be rejected. They will go to Hell.  They will be in pain.  They will be in sorrow.  They will be all alone.  They will be in torment.  They will then be cast into the lake of fire where they will spend eternity.

For there is a way that seems right to these men, but in the end it leads to death.

## About the Author

**2 Corinthians 5:17**

Therefore, if anyone is in Christ, he is a new creation; the old has gone, the new has come!

Tyrone Short is one of those new creations.  After wandering through the desert for over 35 years, he now serves as a witness to the Amazing Grace of the creator of the heavens and the earth.  As salvation comes from the Lord, Tyrone Short has become a receiver of God's Grace.

Tyrone Short now serves the body of Christ as a writer and Christian Reggae Rapper Prince Trog.